ELLE DECOR
PORTFOLIOS

BATHROOMS

Cover: photo © Marianne Haas
Reportage Marie-Claire Blanckaert

Copyright © 2002 Filipacchi Publishing for the present edition
Copyright © 2000 Editions Filipacchi, Société SONODIP – Elle Décoration, for the French edition

Translated from French by Simon Pleasance and Fronza Woods
Copyedited by Matthew Malady

ISBN: 2 85018 732 1

Color separation: HAFIBA

Printed in France by Clerc

BATHROOMS

filipacchi
publishing

Bathrooms. whatever their style—contemporary. classic. unconventional. or rustic—have become fully-fledged rooms in their own right. Refuges. Safe havens. The most private of private rooms. In the 19th century. dressing tables were part of the bedroom. Today. more often than not. it is the bedroom that encroaches upon the bathroom—with sofas. pictures on the walls. wood paneling. and even wall hangings.

In large homes. it is common for people to sacrifice a bedroom to create a large bathroom. But for homeowners who do not have room to spare. the bathtub may end up in their bedroom. where the mirror and sink become part of the decoration.

The truly original among us turn our bathroom into a showpiece of our offbeat tastes.

Lovers of things contemporary can have a field day with minimalism. in pursuit of materials that are at once raw and refined.

This little book is not solely intended to make you dream big. Rather. our hope is that readers will find an idea they can borrow on each and every page.

CONTENTS

BATHROOMS
FOR LIVING IN

BATHROOMS CAN SERVE AS A WELCOMING PLACE WHERE THE PRACTICAL IS MADE PLEASURABLE. WHY NOT IMAGINE A BATHROOM FOR LIVING IN, WHERE YOU CAN ENJOY YOUR SOLITUDE, TAKE TIME TO RELAX IN COMFORTABLE ARMCHAIRS, AND MARVEL AT A MUCH-LOVED PAINTING.

Left. In the London home of interior decorator Anthony Collett, the walls are partly covered by painted paneling. The 1930s' bathtub was found on a construction site. The floor consists of an oak and teak checkerboard. The arts & crafts armchairs have canvas-covered cushions. There is a cabinet behind each mirror. The large painting is by David Champion. **Above.** In this triplex in Lyons, designed by architect Rémi Tessier, the bathroom radiator is hidden behind a woven wooden blind. The floor is covered with sand-colored comblanchien (a type of limestone from eastern France). The walls are painted with marble powder, resembling matt stucco.

Left. In Ireland's Luttrellstown Castle, this bathroom, with its splendid dimensions, calls to mind certain scenes in *Barry Lyndon*. It is as sumptuous as it is comfortable, and reminds one more of a living room—with its two Chippendale wing chairs, its window seats, and chintz curtains. The lion's-paw bathtub, lit by a magnificent chandelier, holds court, so to speak, right smack in the middle of the room.

Above. Another bathroom boasts an amazing 19th century copper tub that has been restored and set in a bay-window adjoining one of the bedrooms. It exudes remarkable elegance for a bathroom.

11

BATHROOMS FOR LIVING IN

In Karl Lagerfeld's home, the morning bathroom looks out over the sea, while the evening one makes the most of the setting sun.

Far left. In the morning, the master of the house shaves in this room, where Anglo-Indian armchairs inlaid with pink coral are the main decorative feature.

Left. For evenings, the Louis XVI-style bath is surrounded by veined marble. The many refined details in this bathroom include the small lyre-backed chair in gilded wood, and the silk Austrian blind.

Left. This immense bathroom, in France's Bagnols castle-hotel, in the Beaujolais region, is filled with rounded shapes. The upper half of the walls are painted in trompe-l'oeil, which serves to emphasize the shape of the bathtub, sinks and mirrors. And the wing chair gives the room the character of a living room.
Above left. The "Taller de Arquitectura," or "Architecture Workshop," in Barcelona, has been converted by Ricardo Bofill so as to combine warmth and friendliness with an atmosphere of contemplation. A low bath has been set into the floor of the bedroom. A triptych of pivoting mirror-shutters can be used to adjust the lighting in the room. The chair on the right is a reproduction of a Gaudi chair.

Above right. Silvio Rech and Chris Browne have decorated the Ngorongoro Crater Lodge, in Tanzania, in a Baroque style. Beyond the long silk curtains lies the savannah. The bathtub is covered in concrete and embellished by a piece of carved wood. Limed wooden paneling is affixed to the walls with large hammered nails. The Medici vase lends a touch of Italian style.

BATHROOMS
FOR LIVING IN

In the home of the famous
Belgian couturier Edouard
Vermeulen, the bathroom has
been designed as a living room,
complete with pouffe and
armchair (Axel Vervoordt)
covered with white linen, and
Louis XVI cabriole chair.
An 18th century parquet has
been chosen for the floor.
The sink unit is in oak, with
the sinks set in black stone.

CONTEMPORARY
BATHROOMS

IN THE CONTEMPORARY BATHROOM, MODERN MATERIALS SUCH
AS SANDBLASTED GLASS, CHROME-PLATED NICKEL, AND RESIN ARE
COMBINED WITH SLATE, GRANITE, AND TRAVERTINE, TO FORM REFINED
LINES OFTEN COMPLYING WITH A CAREFULLY DESIGNED SYMMETRY. THE
HOMOGENEITY OF THE DESIGN IS INVARIABLY A CONSTANT FEATURE, AS
ARE THE BEAUTY OF THE ACCESSORIES AND THE CREATIVE USE OF LIGHT.

Left. In the home of decorator
and designer Agnès Comar.
the bathroom is lit by sunlight
from her private garden.
The sink and bathtub
are set on slabs of green slate.
The floor is pale oak parquet.
The towels are by the designer
herself. and the drawing is
by Suzanne Valladon.
Above. Decorator Jean
de Meulder chose natural
materials to cover the areas
around this bath in an
Antwerp townhouse. The room
is clad in dark green stone
from the Dolomites. as well as
white and green marble. The
bathtub is by Philippe Starck.
The room represents a
harmonious marriage of
minimalism and luxury.

Above left. In Kenzo's home. a
stone's throw from the Bastille.
in Paris. the bathroom is quite
zen. Inspired by a Japanese
wooden bath house. the floor.
walls. and tub are made entirely
of sanded gray granite.
The room opens onto a terrace.
thus creating that particularly
Japanese juxtaposition of
nature and interior.

Above right. Decorator
Anouska Hempel has given
the Hempel Hotel in London
a minimalist aesthetic.
As in all the rooms. she has
here decided to merge oriental
inspiration with architectural
rigor. The tub is in granite.
The view over a private
square adds to the serenity
of the place.

Right. In this house. decorated
by Jean de Meulder. the
bathroom is in the bedroom.
The bathtub is separated
from the sink by an acid-
treated wall of porphyry.
Porphyry is also used for
the rim around the edge
of the tub. The plumbing
fittings are made of
matt nickel.

CONTEMPORARY
BATHROOMS

With its large window opening
onto a natural setting, this
bathroom looks very much like
a studio. This was precisely
what artist Fabienne Villacreces
intended for her home near
Toulouse, in France.
In the middle of the room is a
very lovely bathtub designed
by Philippe Starck. On the right
is a glass unit that belonged to a
dentist in the early 20th century.

Left. Interior decorators M. and J.-L. Mellerio designed their Paris apartment along symmetrical axes, but were also keen to create a warm atmosphere. The bathroom offers a good illustration of this duality. The room, set below the bedroom, is clad in cedar of Lebanon and tiles. Because the area is quite small, the trick was to set the bathtub perpendicular to the wall, thus making room for two sinks.

Right above. Wood is no longer reserved just for rustic atmospheres. In this home, decorators Didier Gomez and Jean-Jacques Ory have used wood in manner that is both modern and stylish. The walls and parquet floor are in cedar. The bathtub and "alcove wall" are in concrete resin. The bathroom is flanked by two dressing rooms.

Right below. In the home of Belgian antique dealer Jean-Claude Jacquemart, the bathtub is in travertine, as are the floor and sink. The tub is set against a wall that separates it from the shower. The faucets have been fitted into the bathroom counter, which also houses the sink. An Ashanti chair is in the foreground.

CONTEMPORARY BATHROOMS

This bathroom, in an old
converted farmhouse,
has been pared down to
a Japanesque-asceticism.
It is the result of
a stylistic exercise undertaken
by the architect Joseph
Dirand. The goal was to
create a bathroom that did
not show any technical
installations. On the wall,
a large mirror hides small
storage units and cabinets,
lights, switches, plugs, and
plumbing fittings.
The bathtub, floor and
sink unit are thick slabs
of Arudy stone, from the
Basque Country.

Above. On the second floor of the "Starck House," the bathroom is all white, and basks in light filtered through Venetian blinds. At once spare and sophisticated, it includes an old-style bathtub, a unit with drawers, a bowl designed by Starck, and a large Venetian mirror from the Galerie San Marco. A Tom Dixon chair stands near the heated towel rack. The banister upright at the far end of the room has been extended by a pole to hold a lampshade.

Above. In Malaysia, the bungalows at the Le Dataï Hotel offer plenty of comfort on the edge of the jungle. The bathtub, fitted into an alcove, is flanked by two symmetrical sinks. The floor, tub sides, and sinks are all made of "balau," the local wood, while the surfaces of the sink units are in white marble from Langkawi, the island where the hotel is located. The keywords of the decoration here are exoticism and refinement.

CONTEMPORARY BATHROOMS

Refinement without ostentation
is the hallmark of this house
in Neuilly-sur-Seine, near Paris,
redesigned by architect
Laurent Bourgois.
The bathroom juggles the
high-tech effects of stainless
steel and sandblasted glass,
while at the same time
combining these modern
materials with much more
classic marble.

Above left. Here, wood once again provides a contemporary ambience. In this home near Paris, decorated by Didier Gomez, cedar gives the bathroom its tone. There are inside shutters on the window, and two sinks are set into the stone top. Rods acting as towel racks are fitted to the front of the unit.

Above right. In the Amangani Hotel in Jackson, Wyoming, the bathroom floor is in sequoia wood. The room opens onto a private terrace. The various refined details include lemongrass soap, bath essences from Bali, and a black marble soap dish. The slatted wooden blinds serve to filter the light steaming in from outside.

Right. This summer bathroom in a house on the Ile de Ré, on France's Atlantic shore, was designed by A. Blanchet, and features double sinks set into an old workbench. Above the wood-clad bathtub, with its cask-like hoops, a teak-framed mirror hangs on the wall. The whole room is lit by small blue pendant lights from Italy.

Above. Interior decorator Anouska Hempel designed this bathroom in Blake's Hotel, in Amsterdam. The tone of the room is set by the soft, glaze-like hues. The reed blind, painted beige and red, complement the white and raspberry of the wicker armchair from the Ivory Coast. The stripes on the walls are hand-painted.

Right. This bathroom in the Devi Garh Hotel in Udaipur. India, features furnishings and trim made of teak. The sinks and surfaces are in white marble. Note the elegance of the bucket-shaped waste-bins—their shiny nickel matching the brilliance of the bathroom fittings.

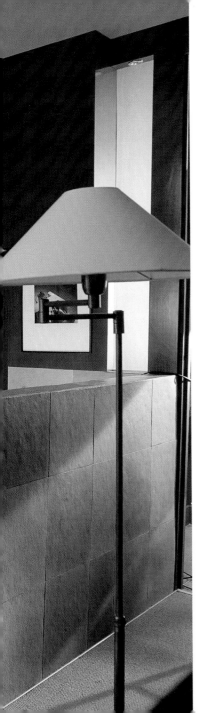

CLASSIC
BATHROOMS

REFINEMENT AND NATURAL MATERIALS ARE THE HALLMARKS OF A CLASSIC BATHROOM. WITH NEITHER OVERPOWERING COLORS, NOR OUT-OF-PLACE EFFECTS, THESE CLASSICS ARE ANSWERABLE TO NO FAD OR FASHION, AND ARE AS APPRECIATED TODAY AS THEY HAVE BEEN THROUGHOUT THE AGES.

Left. Elegance and rigor define this bathroom, decorated by architect Eric Gizard. The furnishings are covered with mahogany veneer while the rim of the bathtub and the floor are of Indian slate. In the back corner, a shower is separated from the main room by a clear glass door.

Above. In the Paris home of Valérie Solvit, director of a communications agency, the twin 1940s' sinks and their period faucets and fittings are topped by antique ebony frames turned into mirrors. She has altered the bathtub by replacing the lion's paws with four large balls.

Left. This Holland Park home in London was decorated by Anthony Collett and Andrew Zarzycki. The bathroom is a celebration of light and beautiful materials. The tiling is marble, and the wooden blinds between the linen curtains filter incoming light. The low armless easy chairs, made by Adnet, are covered with a Canovas terry.

Above left. In the home of Monic Fisher, who established the Blanc d'Ivoire company, the bathroom is completely covered with stoneware tiles. Above the bathtub, there is a shelf holding framed pictures and elephant statues. These decorative items show up well against the contrasting white background.

Above right. This early 20th century town house in Neuilly-sur-Seine, has been totally renovated by architects Daniel and Michel Bismut. The bathroom floor is in combe stone, while the walls and sides of the tub have been given a candle wax finish.

Above. At Luttrellstown Castle, near Dublin, Ireland, this very refined-looking bathroom, with its mahogany-sided bathtub and mahogany-framed mirrors, has the look of a living room—complete with chintz chairs and curtains, here reflected in the mirrors. The sink and accessories are in Victorian style, as are the copper faucets, which have been in this castle for ages.

Above. In Isabella Gnecchi-Ruscone's Paris apartment. decorated by Stéphanie Cauchoix. the paneling is carefully set off by the use of contrasting colors. The black and white panels. Napoleon III table with Scagliola top. and dark carpet with petit point. all strikingly embellish the room. The birdcage in front of the window provides a unique touch.

CLASSIC BATHROOMS

Left. In this winter bathroom on the Ile de Ré, the designer was clever enough to put the bathtub in an alcove. The faucets and lights were found at the Epi d'Or in Paris.

Right. In the middle of this bathroom in the Marrakesh home of Françoise Lafon, the brass sink is set in an all marble unit. The floor and bathtub are also marble, and the tub itself is set into the floor. The engraved glasses and the sink come from Marrakesh street markets. The walls are in "tadlak." A triple mirror by Brot rounds out the room.

Above. This large bathroom has been forged out of two small rooms in a house in Belgium. The space gained made it possible to hide the shower and toilet by creating a wall with the bathtub set against it. Mahogany was used for the furnishings. white marble for the floor. and dark green marble for creating a wide border along the walls.

Above. Decorator Frédéric Méchiche's two-floor apartment in the heart of Paris, exudes the ambience of a country house. To decorate his own bathroom. Méchiche has brought together a collection of early 19th century items, like the bathtub, faucets, grisailles, and flooring. He also added a series of columns, with niches, and a stone stucco stand to raise the tub off the floor. And, no cold feet here—the floor is heated from below.

Above. In this Parisian apartment, antique dealer and decorator Alain Demachy drew his inspiration from the Directoire style. The bathtub has molded wooden sides matching the storage cupboards. The pale shades of color surrounding it show off the old fireplace nicely.

Above. Art director of Marks & Spencer, Brian Godbold, has chosen every detail of the decoration in this cottage in Suffolk, England.

The bathtub is set into painted wooden cladding and flanked by two sinks. The carpet lends a cosy atmosphere to the place.

The armchair is covered with a Charles Hammond fabric. The round and intentionally small mirrors resemble portholes.

47

This bathroom, in the
Strand Hotel in Rangoon,
Burma, uses predominantly
marble and mahogany.
Space, elegant color, a fine
choice of accessories, all help
to create an atmosphere of
luxury and comfort.

Above left. In a museum near Paris that used to be Louis Vuitton's home, a sumptuous sink unit in mahogany has been recycled, complete with its original faucets. This generous and practical piece of furniture is easy to replicate in any kind of wood.

Below left. In one of the bathrooms in a Swiss chalet beside Lake Constance, wood and white marble blend perfectly. The two mirrors are cleverly set in natural wood panes. Although marble is prevalent, it is wood that actually reigns from the floor to the ceiling. The wrought iron lamps were designed by interior decorators Anthony Collett and David Champion.

Right. This bathroom, also designed by Collett and Champion, is made in cherry wood. There is a beautifully realized symmetry, with the sink set in white marble—which also forms the top of the chest of drawers on the opposite wall.

CLASSIC
BATHROOMS

For this bathroom in the
Costes Hotel, in Paris,
Jacques Garcia used old
furniture that he diverted
from its original uses.
The painted cast iron tub is
by Jacob Delafon. The floor
is made of cement tiles.

ECCENTRIC
BATHROOMS

THE BATHROOM REFLECTS THE PERSONALITY OF THE PERSON WHO CREATED IT. AS SUCH, IT ALSO OPENS THE DOOR TO EVERY FANTASY. UNIQUE ROOMS FEATURING DARING SHAPES AND MATERIALS, AN ENDLESS RANGE OF COLORS, AND STUNNING VIEWS FROM THE BATHTUB ARE ALL COMMON PLACES WHEN EXAMINING ECCENTRIC BATHROOM DESIGN.

Far left. In Provence, the daring style of Maxime de la Falaise crops up in this "patchwork bathroom," with its different Carocim cement tiles. Patch the dog takes center stage above the bathtub, which was found at a demolition site's, in—where else?—Bath! On the left, the "Marguerite" chair is upholstered African-style, so as to remain faithful to one of the sources of inspiration for the decoration of the house.

Left. This light and simple space blends well with the rest of Jacques Séguéla's home, which has been remodeled by architect Jean-François Bodin. In the middle of the bathroom, opposite the window, a Jacob Delafon bathtub, with its generous dimensions, sits imposingly. It has been refurbished and painted in imitation marble. The glazed wooden blinds are from Conran's in London.

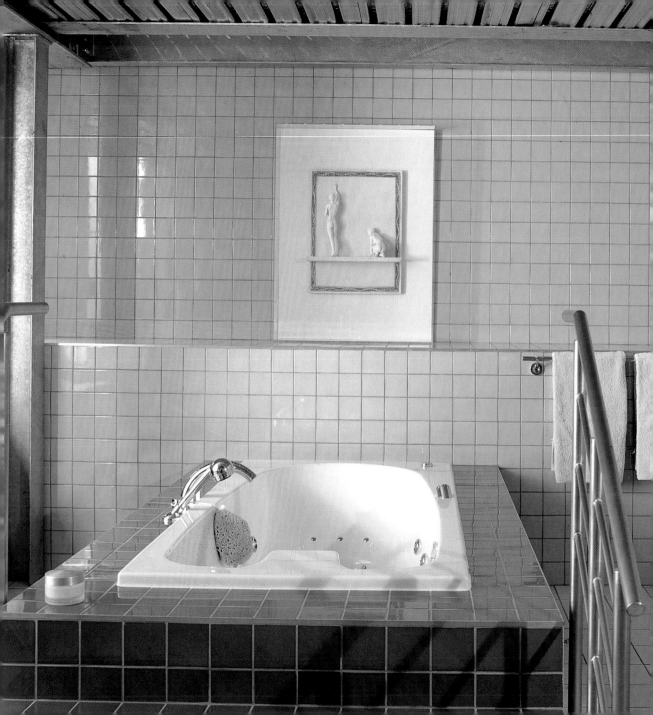

Left. High-tech spirit and industrial aesthetics meet in this loft in Bruges, Belgium. The space was once an abandoned factory, but has been beautifully converted by architect Linda Arschoot. The Jacuzzi tub has been raised to provide bathers with a view over the pool outside. The walls and floor are covered with faience tiles in two shades of green. The sinks and stainless steel faucets and fittings are by Starck.

Above. In Yves Saint Laurent's residence in Marrakesh, the star-shaped bathroom mirror calls to mind the ponds in the Majorelle gardens. The walls are in orangy "tadlak," while the sides of the sink and tub are in green zelliges. Yves Saint Laurent entrusted the decoration and design of his house first to interior decorator Bill Willis, and then to Jacqueline Foissac. The wall lights are in 1930s' style.

ECCENTRIC
BATHROOMS

This unpretentious, modern
bathroom is nonetheless
spectacular thanks to its
"window to the world."
Belgian architect Pierre
Lombart can enjoy
this amazing view over
Johannesburg, South Africa,
either from his bed or from
his bathtub. To make the
most of the truly aerial
positioning of his home,
he chose to focus on the idea
of space—and spaciousness.
The result can be seen in his
decorative choices: simple
materials and sharp lines.

Here is the bathroom of kings in the Ministry of Foreign Affairs in Paris. Two bathrooms were designed in 1938 by the Compagnie des Arts Français to mark the visit of the king and queen of England. The design was done in a very modern vein: spare lines, gold and silver mosaics, chrome-plated pipes, exploded glass.

Left. The king's bathtub features gilded tiles, faucets and handrails. The head of the bath contains a hidden light. Medallions of exploded glass are embedded in the ceiling frieze, and also serve to conceal lights. The floor is in sanded marble.

inlaid with copper scallop-shaped designs.

Above. In the queen's bathroom, the pattern of the Labouré exploded glass wall-piece hides lighting. These creations, by the Compagnie des Arts Français, are reminders of the creative brilliance of artists of the day such as Adnet.

ECCENTRIC
BATHROOMS

Daring and tradition are the
hallmarks of Bettina Bachmann,
an American decorator based
near Oxford, England. In her
bathroom, the walls are painted
blotting-paper pink and apricot,
as are the walls visible through
the door to the right. The side
for the tub was designed by
Bettina and made by the local
blacksmith. The Victorian
chaise longue is covered with
heavy white cotton cloth, and
a jute carpet covers the floor.

COUNTRY
BATHROOMS

TWO OF THE MOST PRIZED PRIVILEGES OF COUNTRY LIFE ARE SPACE
AND NATURAL MATERIALS. PASTORAL COUNTRY SETTINGS INHERENTLY
SPRING TO MIND THE VALUE OF REST AND RELAXATION. AND THE
TRADITIONAL WIDE BATHTUB IS THE IDEAL PLACE FOR LETTING OFF
STEAM, AND ENJOYING A MOMENT TO ONE'S SELF.

Left. Anna and Gunther
Lambert decided to make a
home of this old, 18th century
manor house in Picardy.
The upper walls of this
bathroom are covered with a
beautiful black Jouy fabric,
while the lower part is made
of lacquered white wood.
The Gunther Lambert
armchairs are in black
rattan and wrought iron.

Above. One of the bathrooms
in Yves and Michelle
Halard's castle in the Berry
region, France, has taken
over a room it was not
meant to be in, resulting in
a bathroom with living room
sensibilities. The walls
are covered in a deep red
Jouy fabric. The toilet table
has been improvised from
an old carving table.

COUNTRY BATHROOMS

Left. In Belgium, in the home of advertising executive and collector Marcel Cornille, the marble bathtub placed in the middle of the bathroom comes from a spa, and the faucets from Jermyn Street in London. Above the sinks, the two mirrors are framed in marble. A collector's spirit imbues this Flemish house with its simple, stout architecture.

Right. The attic area of this house on the shores of Lake Constance in Switzerland, has been used to create an amazing bathroom with a bleached pine sloping ceiling. The towel racks are set in a wooden frame that opens onto a cupboard. Anthony Collett and David Champion devised the decoration for the house by opening up the interior space, as much as possible, to the surrounding countryside. Here, two windows offer headlong views of the lake.

Left. The bathroom in this apartment located on the Left Bank in Paris, is in mahogany veneer. The shutter-like doors of the cupboards beneath the sink and the sepia photos of maharajahs emphasize the Anglo-Indian character of the room.

Right above. A bathroom covered in subway tiles is at the heart of a delightful house on Porquerolles Island, on the south coast of France. The whiteness of the walls contrasts with the dark hues of the Ipé wood, and highlights the marine inspiration of the decorations. A large oblong mirror overlooks the tub and sink.

Right below. The laboratory originally designed by Mr. Rockefeller for developing his own photos has been cunningly converted into a bathroom in the Point Hotel in the New York Adirondacks. The slate developing trays have become sinks. On the right, in the mirror, you can glimpse the white-tiled alcove that accommodates the bathtub. The walls, ceiling, and sink unit, are all made of rough pine planking.

COUNTRY BATHROOMS

Inside the beautiful Mont-Blanc
Hotel in Megève, the pine
bathroom was designed
by Jean-Louis Sibuet—
who was responsible for
the renovation of the entire
building—and constructed
by a local carpenter.
The large bathtub has a sink
on either side, set in small
pine units. The result of
Sibuet's work is a room with
Nordic flavor in the middle of
Haute-Savoie, in the Alps.

Left. In Christian Tortu's home in Provence, the window that opens onto a garden courtyard is framed by two old-style kitchen sinks placed on simple wooden planks. An almost monastic, though contemporary atmosphere reigns here. The bathtub is set in a wooden casing.

Right above. This old house in the heart of Brussels features limed teak doors that were inspired by a colonial shutter, and brought back from Thailand. The early 1900s' sink and tub come from England, while the mirror, with its copper molding, was found in a café in southern France. The pair of park chairs of Belgian origin are in stripped fir. Surveying the bathtub is an English model schooner.

Right below. In the castle that they redesigned, at Châteaurenaud, France, Yves and Michelle Halard paid great attention to the bathroom. The parquet is limed in a gray shade which picks out the gray of the walls. The blue stripes of the curtains match the doors and the window. The prints are taken from Diderot's *Encyclopédie*. The bathtub and sink on legs are both antiques.

These three bathrooms are found in Bagnols castle, in the Beaujolais region of France.

Left. In this slightly attic-like space beneath the roofs of a turret, the two window alcoves house a pair of mirrors on old stands. In the middle, dividing the room into two, a bathtub is set in a generous wooden frame.

Right above. The bathtub here is set in a piece of wooden furniture, the upper part of which has been set off by a triple mirror, topped by a cornice.

Right below. A rustic, intimate atmosphere reigns in this bathroom, with its exposed beams and oak sink units. The antique marble bathtub has been set in the middle of the room, and the antique faucet juts from the mirror.

75

COUNTRY
BATHROOMS

In the ski lodge setting,
a rather unusual idea,
the "You and Me" bathroom,
with its two tubs set diagonally
and separated by a wide slat of
wood perfect for holding a
cup of tea, or any other warm
drink, after a long day of
slopes. The window offers a
view of the surrounding
mountains. The walls and the
units for the two sinks are in
fir shuttering. The only
decorative features are wooden
Nepalese milk jugs and
an Indonesian basket.

SINKS
AND SHOWERS

THE ESSENTIAL COMPONENTS OF A BATHROOM ARE SINKS AND SHOWERS.
WHERE THESE ESSENTIALS ARE PLACED VARIES ACCORDING TO THE DESIGNER'S
WHIM. WITH JUST THE SLIGHTEST BIT OF INGENUITY, A DULL BATHROOM CAN
BE TRANSFORMED INTO A COMPLETELY NEW ENVIRONMENT.

Left. The spare lines in the
bathroom of this Parisian
apartment perfectly represent the
minimalist aesthetics espoused
by its designer Christian Liaigre.
A door made of exotic wood
opens onto a sink hewn from
a block of marble.

Above. For the Hempel Hotel
in London. decorator Anouska
Hempel designed this show-
stopper of a sink in Perspex.
The entire bathroom
is lit by a powerful light
embedded in the lower part
of the sink.

Left. In the "Pierre Bergé" suite at the Lutétia Hotel in Paris. the marble bathroom was designed by interior decorator Jacques Grange. The room is highlighted by a sink on its iron stand and the marble paneling that runs around the floor.

Above left. Architect Axel Verhoustraeten decorated this bathroom using flambé blue stone and teak for the floor. and stone for the sink set in a counter top made of wenge. Fine metal mesh blinds hang in front of the small windows.

Above right. In her Chelsea apartment in London. interior decorator Kelly Hoppen has combined the natural with the elegant. A stone bowl is placed on a storage unit. Bathroom cabinets are hidden behind each mirror.

Above left. This George III mahogany corner cupboard, in an Irish castle, has been used to accommodate a small Victorian sink. The copper faucets are the originals. The siphon and plumbing are concealed in the lower part of the cupboard.

Above right. This English pine table has been turned into a bathroom unit. The sink is set in a gray marble top. The white wall tiles have been laid both straight and diagonally to break up the monotony.

Right. In perfume creator Annick Goutal's Parisian house, the laboratory contains a fountain sink in gray stone mounted on cast iron legs. Above it hangs a round zinc skylight window, found in a scrap yard. A mirror with a light has been fitted in the aperture.

Left. This small washbowl has been built into a cherry wood unit. The walls are also done in cherry so the sink blends with its harmonious surroundings. The photograph on the far wall is by Irving Penn.
Above left and center. At the Amangani Hotel in Wyoming,

architect Ed Tuttle designed the various suites with one basic theme in mind: refinement combined with simplicity. All of the materials used have been especially carefully chosen with this notion in mind. The bathrooms are in redwood, with the sinks set in large slabs of slate.

Above right. In a Parisian hotel near Place Vendôme, decorator Jacques Garcia has used antique furniture diverted from its original function. Here the bedpost of a Napoleon III Indio-Portuguese bed accommodates a sink. The floor is covered with cement tiles.

Above left. A sink area—installed in a nook in one of the suites at Blake's Hotel in Amsterdam—was designed by interior decorator Anouska Hempel. The sink is in Portland stone and the Chinese pots match the lacquered paneling.
Above right. At the Point Hotel in New York

Adirondacks. this elongated bathroom puts simplicity first. Sinks. faucets and fittings. shelves. lights. and mirrors are all from the 1930s. Shelves are built into the wall behind the mirrors. A few touches of black interrupt the whiteness of the white tiles.

Right. In the home of communications executive Valérie Solvit. the cement-tiles floor creates a harmony of black and white. The 1940s-style sink is in the same color scheme. The mirror has been pierced to hold the lights.

Above left. A contemporary design was used for this porcelain sink, made to be placed on a piece of bathroom furniture or similar surface.

Above right. In the home of decorator Carole Fakiel, the bathroom walls are covered in ivory-colored industrial ceramic. Two kitchen sinks have been turned into sinks. The faucets are by Stella.

Left. This room in Kenzo's Paris home shows the refinement of a Japanese-style bathroom. The walls are clad with sycamore.

A very small. round sink in marble is set into a surface with a magnifying mirror to one side of it. The two facing mirrors hide the storage units. The small modular openings. and their triangle of canvas fabric. were created by Kenji Kawabata. **Below left.** In the Devi Garh Hotel in India. this small marble bowl with a hole in it is to be used as a sink. It is set on a marble bracket. **Bottom left.** Water pours into a stone bathtub by Boffi. **Below right.** In the home of London antique dealer Gordon Watson. the sink. with its antique-style faucets. is a nickel-plated metal bowl placed on a limestone counter.

Left. A beautiful idea
by decorator and designer
Agnès Comar: a chrome-plated
bucket with a hole in it
becomes a sink.

Above. This custom-made sink
is in stainless steel and
set into a teak surface.
It is a touch of Christian
Liaigre's minimalist world.

Right. This round sink in
birch wood, designed to be
placed on a surface or affixed,
displays a great deal of style.
It also comes in wenge.

Right page. Inspired by old
toilet tables, Philippe Starck
came up with this design for
Duravit. The table is in stained

pear wood, and the bowl is
placed on a thick ceramic sla
The Axor Starck chrome-pla
mixer faucet, a Starck desig
is made by Hansgrohe.

Above left. In an apartment designed by David Champion and Anthony Collett, the shower is enclosed behind a simple glass door, thus creating an actual cubicle. The bath towels hanging on the heated rack are within easy reach.

Above right. For this triplex by the Bois de Boulogne in Paris, decorator Yves Taralon used the natural transparency of glass and the natural simplicity of wood. The bath side is in goyabon, a wood from Brazil, and the floor is in limestone.

Right. In the home of architect Aude Cardinale, in the sauna and spa area, a large iroko tub is set on the stoneware tiled floor. The tiles are hemmed by pebbles set in concrete.

Left. The double shower in this Antwerp home, is lit from the sides, giving the water a rather magical look as it gushes out of large shower heads. The walls are in flambé gray granite. The design is by interior decorator Jean de Meulder.

Right. In Luttrellstown Castle, in Ireland, this bathroom feature a most unusual bathtub fitted with a Jacuzzi and a shower. This type of sanitary installation was once used in monasteries. The concept originated from Victorian days.

ACCESSORIES

MIRRORS, FAUCETS AND FITTINGS, TOWEL RAILS AND RACKS, LIGHTS—
ALL VITAL COMPONENTS WHICH PROVIDE THE FINISHING TOUCHES
TO A BATHROOM, BE IT CLASSIC OR CONTEMPORARY. ALTHOUGH
THEY ARE PRACTICAL ABOVE ALL ELSE, ACCESSORIES CAN BE VERY BEAUTI-
FUL, AND ARE SOMETIMES DESIGNED IN SURPRISING MATERIALS.

Left. This bathroom displays
some classic accessories.
It features a brass and bronze
wall-mounted towel rack.
a two-sided mirror on a stand
with a Brot gilded finish.and
a gilded faucet and
fittings element
with shower head rest.
Also present are a wall soap
dish and a ball hook in polished
brass. The ball is in Perspex.
The brass wall fitting bar
is in varnished polished brass.
Above. For the bath and
shower, a fine example
of elegant. practical.
nickel-plated faucet and
fittings. It stands out well
against a wall covered with
a mineral-based rendering.
in the Italian stucco style.

ACCESSORIES

The successful marriage of glass and metal:

1. Vertical light in nickel-plated metal and sandblasted glass.

2. 10. 14. Globe wall lamp in nickel-plated metal and frosted glass. towel ring and wall soap dish in white opaline. There are also matching faucets and fittings.

3. 4. Square dish in silver-plated metal. and satin-finished glass bottle.

5. Chrome-plated glass soap dish.

6. Gilded. wall-mounted sponge-holder in fine gold. with natural sponge.

7. 9. Nickel-plated hat hook. and pivoting lamp with conical streaked glass shade.

8. Muguet bottle in crystal.

11. Silver-plated porcelain cup.

12. Tooth brush with faux-metal finish.

13. Canted. chrome-plated metal bar.

15. Nickel-plated oval tidy.

16. Green. enameled ceramic tiles.

Left. Solid, nickel-plated brass hook, designed by Andrée Putman. Solid, chrome-plated brass cabochon bathrobe peg. Turned nickel and Perspex ball hook.

Below far left. Pivoting, two-sided chrome-plated mirror—one magnifying side.

Below left. Art Deco electric towel rack in chrome-plated steel.

Right. Corner soap dish in solid, chrome-plated brass, for fixing to the wall. Double-bottomed soap dish in chrome-plated brass. Wall soap-dish in nickel-plated brass, by Andrée Putman.

Below. Soap dish on a stand, in chrome-plated metal and opaline.

Left. "Decoradiator," in nickel-plated brass, that can be connected to a central heating or electrical system.

Below. Towel rack on stand, in nickel.

Top right.
Linen rack in nickel-plated brass and Perspex, by Andrée Putman.

Bottom right: a, c, d.
Towel rack and two wall soap dishes in nickel-plated brass. **b.** Pivoting towel rack in Perspex and nickel-plated brass.

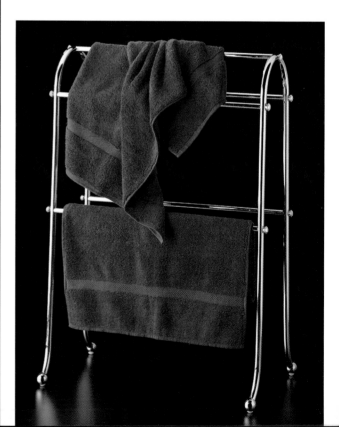

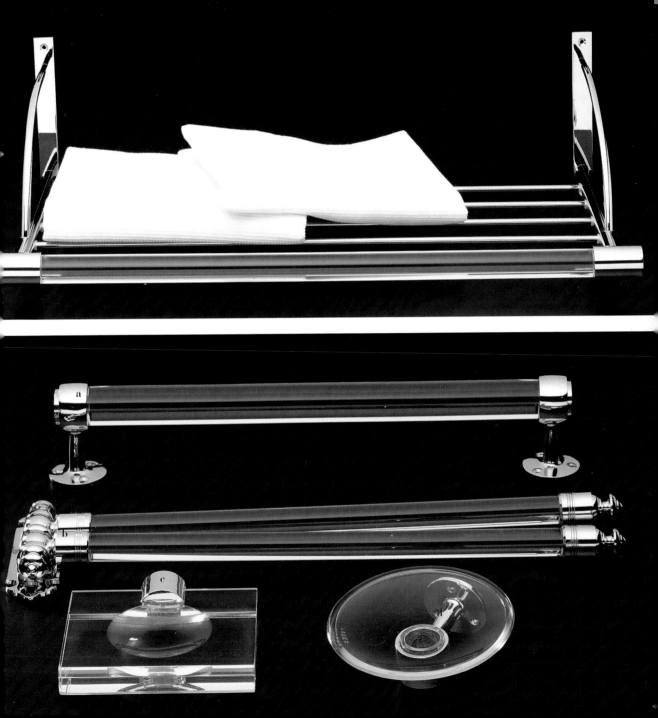

Far left. In a bleached-pine setting created by Anthony Collett and David Champion, the white marble sink is set off by a pivoting mirror in polished nickel, and lit by a light of the same material. The bathtub is reflected in the mirror.

Left. The furniture and walls in this bathroom are in bleached, brushed oak, and the sink counter is in Cascaie blue. The pivoting mirror was designed by Belgian architect Axel Verhoustraeten. The faucets and fittings are by Czech & Speake.

Left.

1. Cherry wood unit. Faucets and fittings, washstand surface in glass and stainless steel sink, and cabinet with drawers.

2. Soap dish on stand.

3. Shaving brush and razor.

4. Metal bottles.

5, 6. Soap box and brush.

7. Chestnut basket.

8. Cologne bottles.

9. Sponge.

10. Coconut fiber brushes.

11. Cherry wood box.

12. Linens.

Right.

1. Small storage stand in chrome-plated metal, designed in the early 20th century in Vienna.

2. Chrome-plated shampoo bottle.

3. Soap dish in frosted glass.

4. Alum stone.

5. Blown glass bottles with silver-leaf decoration.

6. Hairbrushes.

7. Nickel-plated brass hook.

8. Terry cloth towels.

FLOORS & WALLS

BEFORE INSTALLING SINKS, SHOWERS, AND BATHTUBS, IT IS ADVIS-
ABLE TO CHOOSE THE MATERIALS THAT WILL COVER YOUR BATHROOM
WALLS AND FLOOR. CERAMICS, FAIENCE, AND MOSAICS CAN RESULT IN
PANORAMAS OF ENDLESS COMBINATIONS.

Left. This bathroom, designed in 1930's style, is a fine example of an interplay between patterns and reflections. It combines the charm of an old-style design with modern comfort. The white enameled tiling with diagonal black cabochons stands out due to its bareness. The bathtub is tucked away behind a sliding-glass panel.

Above. An idea: combine basic tiles with fillets, friezes, and cabochons.
1. Tracerywork, tinted cement tile.
2. Stone tiles in beige colors.
3. Aged marble octagon and cabochons.
4. Patinated stone, frieze.

FLOORS & WALLS

Ceramic, marble, terra cotta,
and new cement tiles.
1. 4. Slightly ochreish
cement tiles laid diagonally.
2. Alicanth red tiles in polished
marble, with matching border.
3. Stoneware, composition of
octagonal tiles, and cabochons.
5. Terra cotta tile inlaid with
a motif in white enamel.
6. Hand-crafted, talcked terra
cotta and white terra cotta.
7. Large pink ochre tiles in
terra cotta.
8. Subtle shades for
these small, colored tiles.
9. Checkerboard of terra
cotta tiles.
10. Same-colored cement tiles
to be rounded off with a line of
tiles with patterns so as to create
edges and motifs.
11. Star-shaped rosette made
with lozenges and hexagons in
white terre de France.
12. 13. Enameled
sandstone, patinated stone
decor or polished marble.

FLOORS & WALLS

1. Crackled industrial tiling.
2, 3, 4. Tile, lozenge, and edging of hand-crafted enameled terra cotta for floors, bathrooms and walls.
5. Checkerboard of enameled clay tiles.
6, 7, 8, 9. Hand-crafted, enameled terra cotta for walls, molding, corner piece, tiles, and frieze.
10. Square and navette-shaped hand-crafted terra cotta tiles.
11. Industrial enameled sandstone.
12, 14. Matt white, wide choice of sizes in enameled sandstone.
13. Small, molten glass tiles for frieze or mosaic.
15. Faience, industrial tiling.
16. Mottled effect in monochrome, industrial tile of enameled sandstone.
17. Glossy white, faience tiles for walls.

FLOORS & WALLS

Enameled ceramics for countless
different wall friezes.
1, 2. Wide zellige, and tiles.
3. White, bevelled tiles with
two fillets, edging, and molding.
4. Leaf motif, fronton.
5. Tile in matt beige sandstone,
and marble frieze with ivy
carving.
6. Acanthus frieze, and hand-
crafted tile.
7. Tile and matching fillet.
8. Natural stone in frieze,
ceramic.
9, 15. Small, plastic tiles.
10, 17. Square tiles for floors
and walls.
11. Wall combinations: octagons,
cabochons, and molded fillet.
12. Reproduction, 16th century
Italian, ivy frieze.
13. Fine crazing or accentuated.
14. Moorish-style edging
and tile.
16. Molding, ivory white tile.
18. Tile with "parsley" patterns.
19. White bevelled tile and
checkerboard frieze.

FLOORS & WALLS

With friezes, picture rails, and
cornices, all types of finishes
are possible.
1. White cable molding.
tiles of enameled terra cotta.
2. In relief, rough terra cotta
frieze.
3. Frieze in red Verona
marble, with ivy carving.
4. Fine fillets in gilded
terra cotta.
5. Enameled terra cotta
moldings with sculpted
leaf motifs.
6. Antique pink, carved marble
frieze and corner piece.
7. Marble mosaic for frieze.
8. Piece in antique white
enameled terra cotta to be
dovetailed to form a frieze.
9, 10, 11. Set of enameled
terra cotta pieces for making
finishes, broad moldings, and
corner tile, picture rail, cornice.
12, 13. In enameled sandstone,
lozenges for making a two-
colored frieze, and cabochons.

FLOORS & WALLS

Terra cotta covers our floors and walls with southern ochres.

1. Brown clay. Tile. and white and brown cabochons.

2. 4. Terra cotta navettes and triangles. with matching tiles.

3. Stone and clay. Octagon and cabochons.

5. Eleven shades of clay. To be mixed or laid in monochrome.

6. White clay. Hexagons and lozenges.

7. 8. Pinkish clay. Tile and relief garland molding. for the wall.

9. Acanthus leaves. Terra cotta for the wall.

10. Mixed clay. Northern Italian tile.

11. Cable moldings. Terra cotta fillets.

12. Tiles. skirting. and frieze in terra cotta.

13. Simple molding in terra cotta for the wall.

14. Handmade tiles in terra cotta.

15. With palmettes. Cement tile with black palmettes. and plain creamy white.

16. Mass-colored cement.

Useful Addresses

GENERAL EQUIPMENT FOR BATHROOMS

AMERICAN STANDARD & PORCHER
(FIXTURES, FURNITURE)
www.us.amstd.com
P: 800-223-0068

ANN SACKS
(FURNITURE, FIXTURES, LIGHTING)
www.annsacks.com
P: 800-278-8453

BOFFI
(FURNITURE, PLUMBING)
www.boffi.com
P: 212-431-8282

COLOMBO
(BATH DESIGN)
www.orionhardware.com
P: 800-226-6627

CZECH AND SPEAKE
(PLUMBING)
www.czechspeake.com

DELTA
(PLUMBING)
www.deltafaucet.com
P: 800-345-3358

DORNBRACHT
(FITTINGS, ACCESSORIES)
www.dornbracht.com
P: 800-774-1181

DURAVIT
(PLUMBING, TUBS, PHILIPPE STARCK DESIGN)
www.duravit.com
P: 888-387-2848

GROHE
(FITTINGS)
www.groheamerica.com
P: 630-582-7711

HANSGROHE
(SHOWER EXPERTS)
www.hansgrohe-usa.com
P: 800-719-1000
(toll-free literature)
P: 800-334-0455
(toll-free customer service)

JACUZZI
(JACUZZI)
www.jacuzzi.com
P: 800-288-4022

KOHLER & KALLISTA
(PLUMBING, BATH DESIGN)
www.kohler.com
P: 800-4-KOHLER
www.kallista.com
P: 888-4-KALLISTA

KWC FAUCETS
(PLUMBING)
www.kwcfaucets.com
P: 800-KWCFCTS

LEFROY BROOKS
(PERIOD-PIECE BATHROOM DESIGN, PLUMBING)
www.lefroybrooks.com
P: 212-226-2242

MIROIRS BROT
(MIRRORS, ACCESSORIES)
www.frenchreflection.com
P: 800-421-4404

MOEN
(BATH DESIGN)
www.moen.com
P: 800-BUY-MOEN

ROBERN
(FURNITURE, ACCESSORIES)
www.robern.com
P: 800-877-2376

STEAMASTER
(HOME SPA)
www.steamist.com
P: 201-933-5800

SUB-ZERO/WOLF
(PLUMBING)
www.subzero.com
P: 800-222-7820

TOTO
(FITTINGS, ACCESSORIES)
www.totousa.com
P: 800-350-8686

URBAN ARCHAEOLOGY
(FURNITURE, FIXTURES,
ACCESSORIES, LIGHTING)
www.urbanarchaeology.com
P: 212-431-4646

WATERWORKS
(FURNITURE, FIXTURES,
ACCESSORIES,
LIGHTING, TILES)
www.waterworks.com
P: 800-998-BATH

ACCESSORIES

AD HOC
(ACCESSORIES, BEAUTY)
www.adhocny.com
P: 212-982-7703

CALVIN KLEIN
(ACCESSORIES, LINENS)
P: 800-294-7978
(store locations)
P: 800-256-7373
(order number)

CHAMBERS
(LINENS, ACCESSORIES,
FURNITURE)
P: 800-334-9790

FRETTE
(ACCESSORIES, LINENS)
www.frette.com
P: 800-35-FRETTE

GINGER
(ACCESSORIES, LIGHTS,
HARDWARE)
www.gingerco.com
P: 888-469-6511

LABRAZEL
(FURNISHINGS)
www.labrazel.com

OGGETTI
(ACCESSORIES)
www.oggetti.com
P: 305-576-1044

PORTHAULT
(ACCESSORIES, LINENS)
www.dporthault.fr
P: 212-688-1660

POTTERY BARN
(ACCESSORIES)
www.potterybarn.com
P: 888-779-5176

PRATESI
(ACCESSORIES, LINENS)
www.pratesi.com
P: 800-332-6925

RALPH LAUREN
(BATHWARE,
ACCESSORIES, TEXTILES)
www.rlhome.polo.com
P: 888-475-7674

RESTORATION HARDWARE
(HARDWARE, FURNITURE, ACCESSORIES, TEXTILES)
www.restorationhardware.com
P: 888-243-9720

THE CONRAN SHOP
(BATHWARE, ACCESSORIES, FURNITURE, TEXTILES)
www.conran.com
P: 866-755-9079

WAMSUTTA/SPRINGS
(ACCESSORIES, LINENS)
www.springs.com
P: 888-WAMSUTTA

WHITE HOUSE
(LINENS)
www.the-white-house.com
P: 888-942-7528

TILES

AMTICO
(GLASS, MOSAICS, SHELL, CERAMIC, MARBLE)
www.amtico.com
P: 800-268-4260

ANN SACKS
(STONE, MOSAICS, GLASS, PORCELAIN)
www.annsacks.com
P: 800-278-8453

ARTISTIC TILE
(STONE, GLASS, MOSAICS, CERAMIC, PORCELAIN)
www.artistictile.com
P: 800-260-8646

BISAZZA
(GLASS MOSAICS)
www.bisazzausa.com

COUNTRY FLOORS
(STONE, TERRA COTTA, MOSAICS)
www.countryfloors.com
P: 800-311-9995

DUPONT
(TILING)
www.corian.com
P: 800-4-CORIAN

EMAUX DE BRIARE
(ENAMELED TILES)
www.emauxdebriare.com
P: 516-931-6924

HASTINGS TILE
(STONE, MOSAICS, GLASS, PORCELAIN)
www.hastingstilebath.com
P: 516-379-3500

PARIS CERAMICS
(CERAMIC)
www.parisceramics.com
P: 888-845-3487

WALKER ZANGER
(STONE, CERAMIC)
www.walkerzanger.com
P: 877-611-0199

BEAUTY

AQUA DI PARMA
(CANDLES, SKINCARE)
www.aquadiparma.com
P: 800-777-0087

COTE BASTIDE
(SOAPS, CANDLES)
www.fourseasonsproducts.
com
P: 800-555-8082

DIPTYQUE
(CANDLES, SCENTS)
www.aedes.com

FRESH
(SKINCARE, BODY CARE)
www.fresh.com
P: 800-FRESH-20

KIEHL'S
(SKINCARE, BODY CARE)
www.kiehls.com
P: 800-KIEHLS-1

LAFCO
(BODY CARE, FRAGRANCE,
CANDLES)
www.lafcony.com
P: 800-362-3677

LAURA MERCIER
(SKINCARE)
www.lauramercier.com
P: 888-MERCIER

SPACE NK
(BEAUTY CARE)
www.spacenk.com
P: 800-558-1855

WATERWORKS
(PERSONAL CARE LINE)
www.waterworks.com
P: 800-998-BATH

Photos credits:

Guillaume de Laubier: pp. 8, 10, 11, 14, 16, 17, 19, 21, 29, 36, 38, 39 left and right, 40, 46 to 49, 50 bottom, 51, 54, 56, 65, 67, 70, 71, 73 bottom, 74-75, 79, 81 left and right, 82 left and right, 84, 88 top left, 90 bottom right, 92 left, 93–95, 104, 105.
Marianne Haas: pp. 9, 12, 13, 20 right, 32 right, 34, 41, 43, 44, 50 top, 52-53, 57, 60–63, 69 bottom, 76-77, 80, 85 left, center and right, 86 left, 108.
Gilles de Chabaneix: pp. 20 left, 24, 33, 37, 42, 69 top, 72, 83, 87, 88 bottom, 90 bottom right, 92 right.
Patrice Pascal: pp. 30, 31, 91, 96–99, 106-107, 109–119.
Jacques Dirand: pp. 15 center, 25 top and bottom, 26–28, 32 left, 45, 55, 73 top, 86 right, 89 right.
Deidi von Schaewen: pp. 35, 58, 59, 89 top left.
Philippe Costes: pp. 88 top right, 89 bottom left.
Anne-Françoise Pélissier: pp. 78, 90 top right.
Fabrice Bouquet: pp.100–103.
Vincent Knapp: pp.18, 90 left.
Gilles Trillard: p. 68.
Eric d'Hérouville: p. 15 right.
Daniel Kessler: p. 64.
Alexandre Bailhache: p. 66.

Reportages and production:

Marie-Claire Blanckaert: pp. 8–11, 14, 16–19, 20 right, 21, 25 top and bottom, 26, 27, 29, 32 left and right, 34–39 left and right, 40, 43, 45–49, 50 top and bottom, 51–54, 56, 57, 60–65, 67, 68, 69 bottom, 70–73 top and bottom, 74–77, 79, 80, 81 right and left, 82 left and right, 84, 85 right, center and left, 86 left and right, 87, 88 top to left, 90 left and bottom right, 92 left and right, 93–95, 104, 105.
Misha de Potestad: pp. 91, 97–99, 109–119.
Barbara Bourgois: pp. 28, 30, 31 (text by Gérard Pussey), 33, 42, 69 top, 96, 100–103.
Catherine Scotto: pp. 88 top right, 89 bottom left, 106, 107.
François Baudot: pp. 12, 13, 15 center, 28, 41, 108.
Francesca Cavazzocca: pp. 78, 90 top right.
Marie-Claude Dumoulin: pp. 20 left, 28, 88 bottom.
Olivier Chapel-Stick: pp. 58-59.
Laure Verchère: pp. 22, 23.
Françoise Labro: pp. 44, 55.
Alexandra d'Arnoux: p. 24.
Marie Kalt: p. 89 right.
Brigitte Forgeur: p. 66.
Laurence Dougier: p. 15 right.
Andréa Lucas-Pauwels: p. 28.
Elsa Simon: p. 83.

Elle Decor (U.S.) and *Elle Decoration* (France) are both imprints of the Hachette Filipacchi group.
The content of these books was taken solely from *Elle Decoration* and appeared only in France.

WE WOULD LIKE TO THANK THE OWNERS, DECORATORS, INSTITUTIONS OR HOTELS THAT HAVE WELCOMED *ELLE DECOR* COLLABORATORS FOR THEIR REPORTAGES:

AMANGANI HOTEL (WYOMING, UNITED STATES). LINDA ARSCHOOT. BETTINA BACHMANN. DANIEL AND MICHEL BISMUT. MICHEL BLANC. A. BLANCHET. JEAN-FRANÇOIS BODIN. RICARDO BOFILL. LAURENT BOURGOIS. CHRIS BROWNE (NGORONGORO CRATER LODGE, TANZANIA). STEPHANIE CAUCHOIX. AUDE CARDINALE. DAVID CHAMPION. CHATEAU DE BAGNOLS (BEAUJOLAIS). ANTHONY COLLETT. AGNES COMAR. MARCEL CORNILLE. DATAÏ HOTEL (MALAYSIA). ALAIN DEMACHY. AHMET AND MICA ERTEGUN. CAROLE FAKIEL. MONIC FISHER. JACQUELINE FOISSAC. ERIC GIZARD. ISABELLA GNECCHI-RUSCONE. BRIAN GODBOLD. DIDIER GOMEZ AND JEAN-JACQUES ORY. ANNICK GOUTAL AND ALAIN MEUNIER. ESTHER GUTMER. MICHELLE AND YVES HALARD. ANOUSKA HEMPEL. KELLY HOPPEN. DIDIER LEFORT AND LUC VAICHERE. HÔTEL FRANCE ET CHOISEUL (PARIS, JACQUES GARCIA). HÔTEL LUTETIA (PARIS, JACQUES GRANGE AND PIERRE BERGE). HÔTEL MONT-BLANC (MEGEVE, JOCELYNE AND JEAN-LOUIS SIBUET). JEAN-CLAUDE JACQUEMART. KENZO. MAXIME DE LA FALAISE. FRANÇOISE AND ANDRE LAFON. KARL LAGERFELD. ANNA AND GUNTHER LAMBERT. CHRISTIAN LIAIGRE. PIERRE LOMBART. LUTTRELLSTOWN CASTLE (DUBLIN, IRELAND). JOHN MAC LEOD. FREDERIC MECHICHE. MADO AND JEAN-LOUIS MELLERIO. JEAN DE MEULDER. MINISTRY OF FOREIGN AFFAIRS. ELIE MOUYAL. ANUPAM PODDAR AT THE DEVI GARH HOTEL (UDAIPUR, INDIA). YVES SAINT LAURENT. DANIEL SCHAFFENEERS. JACQUES SEGUELA. CLAUDIO SILVESTRIN. VALERIE SOLVIT. PHILIPPE STARCK. STRAND HOTEL (RANGOON, BIRMANIA). YVES TARALON. THE POINT HOTEL (ADIRONDACKS, UNITED STATES). REMI TESSIER. CHRISTIAN TORTU. AXEL VERHOUSTRAETEN. EDOUARD VERMEULEN. FABIENNE VILLACRECES. GORDON WATSON. ANDREW ZARZYCKI.

Under the direction of
Jean Demachy

Editorial
Marie-Claire Blanckaert

Art Direction
Anne-Marie Chéret

Editing
Claire Cornubert

Photo research
Sandrine Hess